WHAT'S UP
Vocabulary for Those New to America

Jimmy Gyasi Boateng

What's Up
Vocabulary for Those New to America
Copyright © 2022 by Jimmy Gyasi Boateng

All rights reserved. No part of this publication may be reproduced, distributed, or transmitted in any form or by any means, including photocopying, recording, or other electronic or mechanical methods, without the prior written permission of the publisher or author, except in the case of brief quotations embodied in critical reviews and certain other noncommercial uses permitted by copyright law.

Although every precaution has been taken to verify the accuracy of the information contained herein, the author and publisher assume no responsibility for any errors or omissions. No liability is assumed for damages that may result from the use of information contained within.

Library of Congress Control Number: 2022902910
ISBN-13:   Paperback: 978-1-64749-705-7
           Epub: 978-1-64749-706-4

Printed in the United States of America

GoToPublish LLC
1-888-337-1724
www.gotopublish.com
info@gotopublish.com

Preface

The idea behind this book is to make the reader aware of slang expressions used by typical Americans. Although some people might have attended institutions of higher education in their native countries, when they come to America, often they are baffled or confused by American slang, whether consciously or unconsciously. Most of my friends who went to college before coming to America also have problems because they don't let go of their understanding of the local American lingo.

Even though I came from a country—Ghana—whose official language is English, (we were colonized by the British), I had a very hard time understanding the Americans' use of the informal English language. Statements like, "Are you nuts?" meant a whole different thing to me until after I had been here for a while and then I began to decipher what the subtle meanings of these slang expressions are when it comes to the American dialect.

I began to compile these American expressions and put them together in book form so that people who are new to this country might appreciate and understand what they mean. It is my hope that this small book will help both Americans and new immigrants alike, basically by learning these expressions, using them when appropriate, and knowing when not to use expressions that may "rub people in America the wrong way."

ACKNOWLEDGMENTS

Special thanks to God for giving me the wisdom, motivation, and strength to write this book. I also want to thank the workers of Microfibers Inc. in Pawtucket, Rhode Island, with whom I have worked for twenty-five years. There is also a debt of gratitude owed to my colleagues at Gillette Stadium and the New England Patriots (one of the best franchises in the National Football League) with whom I have also worked.

There are some friends who deserve mention, especially Doumato Doumato; Mr. Raul Gonzalez, CEO of Millenium Enterprise of Rhode Island, U.S.A.; Mr. K. Gyasi of Royalboat Enterprise of Ghana; Mr. Kwamina Mends; Lawrence Boateng who lives in England; the entire Yokoman Abusua; and the Bonwire Kente family, who raised me.

I also want to thank Mr. John Osei and family; Mr. Seth Asiamah and family; Mr. Alex Odonkor; Abusua Panin Nana Owusua of Canada; Busy Bee of Pawtucket, my typist; Mr. and Mrs. Martin Kofi Bannerman; my wife, Abena Agyeiwaa; and my children Akosua Boatemaa, Gloria Boateng, and Erica Gyasi Prempeh.

Others who deserve my gratitude include Mr. Alex Danso and family; Mr. and Mrs. Opoku Mensah; Mr. and Mrs. Olu Adenegan; Nana Kwakye Amoah; Mr. and Mrs. Richard Safo; Mr. and Mrs. Alfred Ababio; as well as Deacon Ralph Simmons of Pond Street Baptist Church; Sister June McRae; and Sam Boadu and family. I want to thank my elder brother Mr. George Yaw Boateng (my mentor), and his family who live in London, England.

Finally, I appreciate the support of the Ghanaian community of Providence and vicinity, Boston, and Connecticut. I give special thanks to my ex-wife Sheila Boateng; may God bless her, wherever she may be.

Thank you for reading this book. Put a smile on your face and God bless you. I love you all.

About the Author

Jimmy Gyasi Boateng was born and raised in Bonwire, the historical Kente cloth town of Ghana. I attended Phillips Commercial College in Kumasi, Ghana and after graduation came to Accra, the capital of Ghana, to find a job. I was fortunate enough to be hired by the Parliament House, National Assembly, as a clerical officer, where I worked with Dr. Kwame Nkrumah, the first President of Ghana.

When the Nkrumah administration was overthrown, I continued to work with the second government of Ghana, led by Dr. Kofi Busia and his administration. I remained in this employment with Parliament for ten years before taking a new position with the State Insurance Corporation of Ghana as a librarian.

I came to the United States in 1978 and worked in several factories and institutions, among them Microfibres Corporation. I was chosen as the Associate of the Year in 1996. I have been a loyal employee of the company for twenty-five years.

In addition to working with Microfibres, I have worked for the Massachusetts judiciary for eight years as an interpreter through Inlingua of Boston, and I continue to work with Team Ops of the New England Patriots Football Team at Gillette Stadium in Foxboro, Massachusetts.

I continued my education with a senior high school equivalency diploma from Cranston West, Cranston, Rhode Island, and continued at Rhode Island Trade Shops School, where I graduated in 1982. I furthered my education at Genesis Center with a diploma in Culinary Arts in 2002. Additionally, I hold a certificate from the New England Gerontology Academy.

Introduction

I came to the United States during the Disco era, and I was thrilled to be in this country during those times. One day I went to the store to buy suspenders to look good at the club that played disco music.

When I went to a store to buy the suspenders, I asked the associate working there where I could find braces, because that is what we called suspenders in Ghana. The associate told me to go to the dentist; braces were not sold in department stores. When this misunderstanding took place, I had no knowledge of how people were supposed to talk in the United States. I made a promise to myself not to look stupid again and learn the language.

There was another occurrence when the language barrier came into play. This happened when I went to a college cafeteria to eat. After I got my food, I asked the guy next to me where I could find the cutlery. When I asked for the cutlery, he replied by saying, "What?"

I asked him again where the cutlery was, and he said *what* again, and this time, he got angry and told me to speak English. After this happened I said to myself, "Oh, Lord, let there be light." I did not know that in America cutlery is known as silverware. In Ghana, cutlery set is various kinds of knives, spoons and forks.

After living in the States for a while, I took a trip to the old country, Ghana, in West Africa. I visited my sister and she offered me something to drink. I told her I needed soda. She sent the kids to the neighborhood store to get me soda. When the kids went around the whole neighborhood to find me soda, they were unable to get me any soda. My sister told me that the kids couldn't find any soda. Then I asked her if there was any Coca Cola or Pepsi, and she said yes. I realized that the word soda that I learned in the United States does not apply in Ghana, because in the old country soft drinks like Coke and Pepsi are known as a "minerals."

Chapter One:
Greetings and Partings

One thing that makes America so interesting is the greeting. There are many ways to say hello, and I have listed just a few of them below. The most common gesture is the handshake, which is done between men and women. But even that has a lot of variations, depending on the circumstances and how well people know each other. To be on the safe side, newcomers should simply say "hello" and shake hands until they feel more comfortable.

I have also made a separate section in which I have listed greetings and the responses to those greetings.

These various gestures can be used without saying a word, but most people combine them with something spoken from the list that follows:

High five

Low five

Peace sign

Victory Sign

An embrace ... with a tap on the back

Winning team's celebrations.

Funny gestures: some even show their tongue to tease

Greeting	Response
Hi	Hi
Hey!	Hey! (Or, "Hey, yourself!)
What's up?	Nothing much
What's up?	Hanging in there!
Long time, no see	Yeah, how you been?
Hi, John, how you doing?	Doing fine
Hey, Jimmy what's up?	Not much, man.
What's happening, Comfort?	Not much, man
How you doing, brother?	Everything is cool
What's up, buddy?	All is fine
What's cooking?	Nothing much
How are things going for you?	Better, I hope
Holla (Holler)	Holla back
Hi, pal. What's up?	Nothing much
How is it going man?	Same old, same old
How the hell are you doing?	I'm doing okay, I guess
What's happening, Vida?	Everything is cool
Yo!	Yo!

When it's time for two people to go their separate ways, there are also many ways to express that fact to each other. Those listed below are just a few of the most common ways.

Good-byes

- Stay Cool
- Take it easy
- Stay out of trouble
- See you
- Check you later
- Have a nice day (or perfect day, great day, and so on)
- Enjoy your day
- Good luck
- Catch you on the rebound
- See you later
- See you around
- Nice seeing you

Jimmy Gyasi Boateng at JFK Museum

Chapter Two: Translation of American Expressions

In this section I have listed many examples of American expressions along with an explanation for each.

American expressions that I have listed so far will help people from other countries to get a better grasp of American culture.

I thought you were gonna nuke it.
- I guess you thought it was easier than it was.

The hood of the car
- The bonnet of a car

The trunk of a car
- The boot of a car

Joe is in the doghouse with his wife.
- Joe is in trouble with his wife.
- Joe's wife is so upset with him; she is not talking to him.

Anyone with long cornrows will not be allowed in the club.
- All men with braided hair are not permitted entrance to the club.
- There is a dress code to follow before being permitted in the club.

We've got a back-up plan.

We'll try Plan B next.
- If the first plan doesn't work, other plans will be tried.

The work was a drag; I'm all hatched up.

- The work was boring and made me feel tired.

We were never an item.
- We never had a relationship.

He jumped the gun.
- He went ahead of others.

Fag or faggot or queer (All are socially unacceptable terms; avoid them.)
    A gay person or homosexual

Gay
- Men who have sex with men

Lesbian
- Women who have sex with females

Queen
- Female impersonator—female gender

Mr. Gyasi apologizes for Jimmy's dust-up
- Mr. Gyasi apologizes for the altercation with Jimmy.

DMV or Department of Motor Vehicles
- The agency where licenses are given and cars are registered.

Some guys thought "feminism" made them wusses.
- Some men thought that supporting equal rights for women would make them look weak.

She's got big ass words.
- She uses words that are difficult to understand.

Mr. Yeboah is a steeplejack
- Mr. Yeboah works on steeples and other tall objects.

America's number one health problem is not obesity; it's lack of nookie.
- America's biggest health problem is not being overweight; it's not getting enough sex.

He said that lots of women are getting short-changed in the sack.
- He said many women are not being satisfied during sex.

Joe huffs and puffs as he walk the aisles.
- Joe is in poor health and just walking in a store causes him to breathe heavily.

It was not a slam dunk.
- It wasn't easy and required a lot of effort.

He will not mellow out.
- He is unable to relax.

The police called for back-up.
- The police called for help.

The road has a detour.
- The road has a redirection and can't be used.

He is over the edge.
- He can't handle the situation any longer.

I will sue your ass off.

- I will take you to court and get everything you have.

She/he is mean. (Also, she/he is not friendly.)

- She/he is not a sociable person.

He's got a big gut. (He has a pot belly.)

- He is overweight in the stomach area.

He was sentenced to the slammer for two years.

- He had to pay for his crime with two years in prison.

She got off with a slap on the wrist and a small dent in her wallet.

- For her offense, she was charged a small fine (fee).

It's put up or shut up.

- If you don't have anything constructive to say, keep quiet.

The female teacher is mad banging.

- The teacher is a very beautiful woman.

Photo-jack
Photo bomb
Photo bummer

- When someone in the background spoils a picture by acting stupid. (A person who does this is sometimes called a "Photo Whore.")

He worked his butt off yesterday.
He worked his ass off today.

- He stayed busy all day and didn't even take a break

Say what?
- Did I hear you correctly?

Pardon. (When said while in a crowded situation.)
- Sorry, I didn't mean to bump into you.

Catch some Zs
- Get some sleep?

Do you wanna to get busy?
- Are you looking for an argument (or fight)?

Crack up (As in, "That cracks me up.")
- Smile or laugh because something is amusing.

No cover charge
- No minimum purchase required (usually seen at night clubs with entertainment).

Open house party.
- Anyone can attend the party without an invitation.

The house is for sale, and there will be an open house on Sunday between 12–3 pm.
- Anyone interested in buying the house can see it at this time.

If you like that shit, that means you're missing out.
- If you like that sort of thing, then you are missing even better things besides that.

The man and a cop faced off.
- The man and a police officer began to argue.

The money I get keeps my head above water.
- I earn enough to pay my bills.

Why can't you hit me up man?
- I want to be included.

Can you pitch in to help?
- Can you contribute (either with labor or money)?

He has a thick head.
- He does not listen (also said of a person who is stupid).

I'm looking for the son-of-a-bitch who did that.
- I'm looking for the idiot who did that.

You are (so) weird.
- You do the strangest things. (Usually used in a humorous, friendly situation.)

She is gonna chew your ass off.
- She will be so upset, and you are probably in a lot of trouble.
- She will discipline you severely.

I can't put up with this bullshit.
- I can't tolerate this unpleasant situation.

What the hell is the matter with you?

- What's causing you to make mistakes?

It was a time bomb waiting to go off.
- It was a situation just waiting for the right circumstances to make it a real problem.

No way, no how!
- I refuse to do it.

It looks like we dodged a bullet.
- We escaped having something bad happen.

His car was rear-ended.
- His automobile was hit from behind.

Hey, Jerry, eat your heart out.
- Hey, Jerry, look at what I have; aren't you envious?

They're always going after each other's throat.
- They're always fighting.

My life is a living hell.
- My life is miserable.

What's your take on Mr. Mills's first year in office?
- What is your opinion of Mr. Mills's first year in office?

He groped her.
- He grabbed her in an inappropriate place.

Yuck!
- Usually said when something either does not taste good or is likely not to taste good.

He's on my hit list.
He's on my shit list.
- He's made me very mad, and I will not forget about that.

I'm going to the liquor store and get a six pack of beer.
- Beer is sold six in a package or "pack."

That's really messed up.
- Things are not going according to plan.

Why do you sneak up on me?
- Why do you come from behind to frighten me?
- Or someone coming from behind to frighten you.

He went berserk.
- He went crazy, or he wasn't acting rationally.

My brother didn't finish school, but he is street smart. (or "has street smarts.")
- My brother doesn't have a formal education, but he knows how to get along in the world.

He broke the ice today by talking to his brother.
- He took the first step by starting a conversation with his brother..

It is a slap in the face.
- It is an insult.

Forget about the Xs and Os.
- Don't try to be perfect.

The alarm went off.
- It was time to get up and start the day

Alex will not bad-mouth the TV station.
- Alex will not make negative comments about the TV station.

We are banged up.
- We are slightly injured.

He is a shrewd negotiator.
-    He knows how to make deals with people (usually for his own advantage).

How deep is your pocket?
- Financially are you comfortable?

She is a crybaby.
- She is constantly complaining or crying for attention.

You're gonna freak out!
- You will be in shock. (This can be used in both good and bad situations.)

You can get a fine for jaywalking
- You can pay a penalty for not walking where or when indicated.

They will take him out.
- They will kill him.

He knocked him flat.
- Fred hit him so hard he was unconscious.

I like your hair-do.
- I like the way you styled your hair.

He's a nervous wreck.
- He is anxious and is not looking forward to what is planned.

He is sick in the head.
- He is not a mentally stable person.

He is my buddy.
- He is my good friend.

He's in the driver's seat.
- He is the person who is in charge.

It will be slow coming.
- The check will take a while to get here.

He passed on yesterday.
- He died yesterday.

He is a cool cat.
- He is quite a man.

The captain can't jump ship.
- When trouble arises, the person in charge can't avoid the problem.

Number one - #1
- First place.

What was the recipe for yesterday's dinner?
- What are the directions to prepare yesterday's dinner?

Not that I know of.
- I have no knowledge about that.

It's Friday and time to get flicking.
- It's the end of the work week and time for some fun.

Please give him a round of applause.
Give it up, ladies and gents
- Please clap your hands.

We decided to pass the hat to help them out after her accident.
- We asked for a donation of money to help her ....

He is a workaholic
- All he does is work and has no time to do anything else.

I have a sore back and can't work today.
- I have a pain in my back and hurts too much to go to work today.

Price chopper
- One who wheels and deals to get lower prices.

He's a dummy.

- He is someone who is not too bright (in the opinion of the person speaking).

Asshole

Jackass

Dumb Ass

- Someone who is stupid or undesirable or does not work well with others.

I'm gonna rip you a new one.

I'm gonna rip you a new asshole.

I'm gonna rip your head off

- I am going to make you regret your actions.

I'm just chillaxing

- I'm just relaxing.

Whatever!

- I don't care.

You can lean on me.

- You can depend on me.

You should chill out.

- You shouldn't worry so much, relax.

It was a jaw-dropping case.

- It was an astonishing case.

They are rubbing their nose against our ass.

- They are interfering with our business.

He is doing some time in the slammer.

- He is incarcerated for a crime.

It does not hold water.

- Your story does not tell the whole truth.

Her pocketbook was stolen while she was at the store.

- Her handbag (or purse) was stolen while she was at the store.

A buzz saw won't stop the health care bill.

- The health care bill will be approved no matter what.

The Governor's speech will butt heads with the game.

- The Governor's speech will be on at the same time as the game.

He was arrested for a D.U.I

- He was arrested while Driving Under the Influence (being intoxicated/drunk).

The accident was just a fender bender.

- The car accident was not serious.

Sir Jimmy G. Boateng associate of the year 1996. Mr. James McCulloch President and CEO of Microfibres Inc. Pawtucket, Rhode Island, USA.

That was baloney.

It is all crap and nothing but crap.

- That was not the truth.

You bet your ass.

- You can rely on it.

He runs his mouth off too much.

- He talks too much.

Every time I see the tape, I get goose bumps.

- Every time I see the tape, it gives me a funny feeling.

The car is fully loaded—the whole nine yards

- The automobile has all the essentials and more.

The world population includes many crackpots.

- The world is full of people who do not make sense.

You should use the highway to get there faster.

- You should use the main road (motorway) to get to your destination faster.

It's either my way or the highway.

- There is no chance of doing things differently.

That girl is cute

- That girl is pretty.

John has a reputation for being a brown-noser (or brown nose).

John is a yes-man.
- John is known for trying to win favoritism by flattering the boss.

The store used a billboard for advertising.
- The store used a large sign to advertise (placed outdoors and often on high buildings).

He is a loser.
- He is someone who is not successful at anything.

He is a drug addict
- He is a person who depends on drugs and cannot survive without them.

We went to church and met the new Preacher
- We went to church and met the new minister/reverend/pastor.

The sneakers are cute.
- The shoes made of canvas look good.

Let me tell you what is in the magazine—crap.
- The magazine is not interesting enough for you to read

Who wants to sit in the rat race?
- I'm not interested in that situation.

We do not do Mickey Mouse work here.
- We do not do poor quality work here.

That heart attack was a wake up call to stop smoking.
- That heart attack was a warning to stop smoking.

He'll be able to break loose soon.
- He'll be able to leave soon.

He's a freeloader.
He is a bum.
- He feeds off everybody and never pays his way.

That old man is a penny pincher.
- A person who is frugal and watches everything he / she spends.

Miss Hunter shoots off her mouth and tells all.
- Miss Hunter talks too much and cannot keep a secret

I have my hands full with my own stuff.
- I'm overwhelmed with my own problems

He was arrested for being a peeping tom
- He was arrested for peeking into peoples' windows

The politician had a reputation for flip flopping on issues.
- The politician changed his mind frequently.

She ain't shit but she dresses like "500."
-   She's really no one special, but she wears expensive and top of the line clothing.

He is a dirty cop.
- The police officer takes bribes.

He's catching some Zs.
- He is taking a nap.

Go granny go.
- Cheering for grandmother.

Take a walk on the wild side.
- Do something exciting, or something you never did before.

The man who was just released from jail did a U-turn back into the slammer for violating a restraining order.
- He broke the law and went right back to prison.

Is he funny or just a jerk?
- His humor was not appreciated.

With some sessions they start very strong and at the end they are flat.
- They play well at the beginning and tire at the end.

There are twists and turns along the way
- There will be challenges.

Another one bites the dust.
- Another one (person, team, or company, etc.) loses his position or status has expired.

We don't just talk the talk.
- We don't just talk about the situation, we get it done.

Right on the money
Right on the nose
- The right decision was made
- The right answer was given.

Put your money where your mouth is.
- Prove it.

He has a chip on his shoulder
He has an attitude.
- He has a hostile (or aggressive) attitude.

He is mean.
- He is a vicious person.

He gave me a mean face.
- He looked at me with anger in his eyes.

The police suspected he was a Hit Man
- The police thought he was someone who gets paid to kill someone

My friend works at night as a bouncer.
- My friend works at night spots and removes trouble makers.

Don't push your luck!
- You may not like the results the next time.

Mind your own business.

M.Y.O.B.

Keep your nose out of my business.
- Don't interfere with what I am doing.
- Keep your advice (or opinion) to yourself.

Gotta love it.
- It's something you will definitely enjoy.

They arrested her for being a call girl (or whore or prostitute).
- They arrested her for being someone who gets paid for sexual favors.

The madam was also arrested.
- They also arrested the woman who employed women to sexually gratify men.

Anchorman/Anchorwoman
- The person who reads the news on TV.

He is my own man.
- He is true to me.

We bought those at the nickel and dime store (or "five and ten-cent store).
- We bought those at an inexpensive variety store.

The old man had a reputation for being a penny pincher / miser
- The old is extremely careful with spending money.

He has a sense of humor.

- He is jovial and always in good spirits.

He said that when he met Jimmy the two immediately hit it off.
- They had many things in common and enjoyed each other's company

The situation makes me edgy.
- The situation makes me nervous

There is lots of political pushback.
- The politicians do not want to make the change.

How 'bout them Big Apples?'
- i.e. How about those New Yorkers?

Many large cities have a subway train system.
- Many cities have an underground train for transportation.

White collar jobs
- These jobs are typically done in an office.

Blue collar jobs
- These jobs are often found in manufacturing or in the building trades.

I was afraid that she would snitch about me being out all night.
- I was afraid she would tell others about me being out all night.

Pull your pants up
- Pull your bridges up.

She can be such a bitch sometimes.

- She can be a very disagreeable person.

He has some loose screws upstairs.
- Mentally, he is not capable.

Life is nuts enough without dealing with that.
- Life is hard enough without some extra stress.

He is hot-headed.
- He becomes angry very easily.

There is a panhandler on every corner of the city.
- There is a beggar on every corner ….

Mr. Ababio is a big wig.
- Mr. Ababio is an important man in the community.

He grows flowers as a diversion from his job.
- He grows flowers to take his mind off his work.

I heard the company might have a lay-off.
- I heard the company plans to force some employees out of their jobs.

It is their turn under the gun.
- It is their turn to be under pressure.

This is what is happening in your neck of the woods.
- This is what is happening in your city or town.

This is just a wacky winter.

- This is just a very unusual winter.

What did you say your name was?
- I didn't quite hear your name.

The doctors are giving up on him.
- The doctors say he has no chance of recovering

M.A.D.D.
- Mothers Against Drunk Driving

You will get over it and get on with your life.
- Your sadness is temporary and you will soon be able to live your life normally.

Hit the road

Get lost.

Don't let the door hit you on the way out.
- Leave me alone.

You are making a killing.
- You are very successful with your choice.

He is a junkie.
- He is addicted to illegal drugs.

You need a time out after all that work.
- You need to take a rest from what you are doing.

He was stoned.

- He was under the effects of too many drugs.

He beat the shit out of me.
He beat the crap out of me.
He beat the hell out of me.
- He physically abused me very badly.

This year's Super Bowl ads are goofy.
- Some of the ads didn't make sense.

Goofy
- Not too realistic. i.e. silly

They will take their own sweet time to reply to the mail.
- Don't expect a quick answer to your mail.

You are way ahead of the game.
- You are in good position to advance your strategy.

He is ahead of his time.
- He has ideas no one has ever considered before.

She is a street runner.
She is a jogger.
- She exercises outdoors by running.

She took her suit to the cleaners.
- She paid to have her clothes cleaned and pressed.

He took his dirty clothing to a laundromat

- He went to a place where he could use machines to wash his own clothes.

Jimmy is a party animal.

- Jimmy is always looking for a party to go to.

He can be a party freak.

- He is a person that acts obnoxiously at parties.

I have no clue.

- I don't have any idea what you are talking about.

Jimmy G. Boateng and Mayor Buddy Cianci the longest serving mayor in U.S. history of Providence Rhode Island.

The woman employed her fourteen year old daughter as a drug mule.

- The woman used her daughter as a messenger who carries the drugs between dealers.

My guess is he's going for the wallets.

- My guess is he's looking for a donation.

He never takes "no" for an answer.

- He's very persistent.

Jack is an errand boy.

- Jack is a messenger.

I woke up with a hangover from the party.

- I had too much to drink at the party, and it made me sick.

He's completely out of the woods.

- His health has improved, and he is no longer in danger.

I nearly went off on him.

- He upset me so much, I almost confronted him about it.

He is off the wall.

- Mentally, he is not stable; or, his behavior is very bizarre

Wake up and smell the coffee.

- Stop ignoring the obvious.

There is more to the story than meets the eye.

- He is not telling the whole truth.

After the bank robbery, I just didn't have it in me.
- I didn't want to go to that bank after it had been robbed.
- He lost courage and strength.

If you break bread with that group, you can't bail out on them.
- Once you are aware of their secrets, it's too late to leave the group.

Life sucks and then you die.
- Everything in my life has gone wrong, and I don't see it getting any better.

Who calls the shots in this house?
(Also, "Who wears the pants in this house?")
- Who makes the decisions here?

The boss will write you up.
- You will receive a warning letter.

Dummy
- He 's not too bright; he's a fool.

She wears eyeglasses
- She wears lenses to see better.or

She wears sunglasses during the day.
- She wears sunglasses to protect her eyes from the sun.

What is the name of your primary doctor?
- What is the name of the doctor you see on a usual basis?

Practitioner

- A doctor who practices general health problems.

The landlord stopped by to collect the rent.

- The person who owns the property wants to be paid.

Now that you are a homeowner, you have to take care of your own problems.

- Now that you own your own home, you ….

Sanitation Engineer, Garbage Man, Trash Man

- One who collects the garbage on a weekly basis and works for the city.

The police set a trap to catch the Drug Pusher.

- The police had a plan to arrest the one who sells illegal drugs.

Most of the time, people hear DRUGS and they think about illegal drugs.

- If a doctor prescribes a drug it is called medication. There are also medications that a person can buy without a doctor's permission is called over-the-counter medication.

Pharmacist; druggist

- The one who puts together the prescribed drugs, called a "chemist" in Britain.".

Jail House or Prison

- Slammer – Pen – Joint – Can

We are short-handed

- We don't have enough people to do the job.

I did not know this man from Adam.
- I never met the man and never saw him before.

That man may not be on the up and up.
- That man may not appear to be what he claims.

Custodian
- A person who takes care of something; caretaker
- The person who cleans and maintains a building; also called a "janitor."

Seasons (Weather):
- Winter – cold season starts November to March
- Spring – March to May
- Summer – sunshine. Time for fun and vacation June – August
- Fall – That is the time for the leaves to fall, September and October

Underpants
- Underwear

He spent most of his time on the bench.
- He was a reserve player

Where is my billfold?
- Where is my wallet?

She carries a large pocketbook.
- She carries a large handbag (or purse).

I'm going to take a leak.

- I'm going to pee or urinate

I'm going to take a shit/crap.
- I need to have a bowel movement or go to the toilet.

Toilet roll or toilet paper
- Paper used in the toilet area.

The mother asked her little boy if he had a boo-boo.
- The mother asked her child if he had a cut or something that hurts.

Mailman ("Mail carrier" is now preferred.)
- Person who delivers letters to various homes.

Mail
- Letters, ads, bills, etc.

He is living in his father's shadow.
- He is trying to live up to his father's reputation.

That was gross.
- That was disgusting or sickening.

He is too frisky!
- He has a lot of energy. (If speaking about a pet dog.)
- He is only interested in sex. (If speaking about a man.)

The broad has a fat ass.
- That woman's rear is oversized.

How much is my cut?
- How much is my share?

He is my buddy.
- He is my friend.

It's peanuts.
- It is inexpensive.

Hair grease
- Gel; pomade;

Rotary
- Round about

His mother asked him to take out the trash.
- His mother asked him to remove the discarded rubbish.

He put the old papers in the trash can.
- He put the old papers in a container for disposal.

He talks trash.
- He speaks in an insulting manner

Garbage
- Food that has gone bad

Garbage man
- One who collects garbage

He said he grew up in the country.
- He said he grew up far from a city or large town.

She set a drink on the end table.
- She put the drink on a small table at the end of the sofa.

Lamp Stand
- A piece of furniture that a lamp can fit on

Coffee table
- The coffee table is usually placed in front of the sofa.

Couch
- Sofa used to sit on

Bath towel
- Large towel used to dry off after a shower or swimming, etc.

Face cloth
- Small terrycloth used to wash up

Con man
Con Artist
- One who cheats another person

Smart ass
- One who thinks he knows everything

He has gone to heaven

- He passed away ; he died.

That man is handsome.
- That man is extremely good looking.

Those women are beautiful, and their kids are cute.
- Children are referred to as "cute;" women are pretty or beautiful.

Let's get into the swing of things.
Let's get with the program.
- Let's join in.

Screwdriver
- A tool used to install threaded fasteners; "screws."
- A cocktail made with vodka and orange juice.

Don't give me the run-around.
- Don't waste my time with false information.

Duct Tape
- A wide, multi-purpose tape that is very strong.

Wannabe
- A person who wants to be someone they are not; for example, a *wannabe singer*.

Listen up!
- Pay attention; this is important information.

After he lost the money, he was in a whole lot of trouble.

- After he lost the money, he was in for serious consequences.

I do not have a dime to my name.
- I have spent all the money I had.

I wish you would drop dead.
- You hurt me so badly that I wish you would die.

It's just a drop in the bucket.
There is plenty more where that came from.
- There is an enormous amount available, and this is not significant.

Please stay in line.
- Do go ahead of someone who is also waiting

The radio is blasting.
- Enjoying the music

Boom box
- A large wireless radio

City Hall
- The office of the mayor of the city, also various offices pertaining to official matters.

City Council
- A group chosen by the people to govern the city.

You ain't shit.

- You are worthless.

I'm going to pump some gas
- I have to fill up my tank with gas.

I think he's a little cuckoo.
- I think he's a little crazy.

He's nuts.
- He's crazy.

I'm beat.
- I'm tired.

I'm over-loaded at work.
- I have too many things to do at work.

He's loaded.
- He's very wealthy and considered to be rich.
- He's drunk/intoxicated.

He is filthy rich.
- He has so much money he will never be able to spend it all.

Brown is doing a year.
- Brown is in jail for one year.

The judge threw the book at him.
- The judge gave the criminal the maximum sentence for his crime.

Knock it off!

- Stop what you're doing; it's annoying me.

Hell, no!

- Absolutely no

No way, no how!
What part of no don't you understand?

- Absolutely, the answer is no.

Poncho

- A plastic rain coat that is shaped like a square with a head hole in the middle.

It's coming by horse

- It will eventually get here but slowly.

Choo-Choo train

- Children refer to a train as a "choo-choo."

Police digest/Police blotter

- A police report of an incident

Welcome to the club

- You and I have the same problem!

Shiny Duke was here looking for you

- Referring to a gentleman who had no hair.

He was laughing his ass off.

He was laughing his balls off.

He laughed his butt off.

- He couldn't control his laughing.

The drunk driver hit the Jersey barrier.

- He lost control of the car and hit the guard rail (concrete barrier.)

Bimbo

- A woman who is not very intelligent or one who readily goes to bed with a man.

Slut

- A woman who sleeps with many men.

Everybody is bitching about the job.

- Everyone is complaining about the job.

I owe you no less.

- This is the least I can do for you.

Yankee

- A native or inhabitant of New England
- In other countries, especially Mexico, anyone from America is a Yankee.
- This can also mean a member of the New York Yankees' baseball team.

Cowboy

- A ranch worker who rides horseback, usually caring for cattle or horses.

Do not mess with Uncle Sam.

Be careful with the American government.

- Don't try to fool the government. Ex.: Don't cheat on your income tax form.

Latinos

- Spanish-speaking people from various areas of Central and South America (usually Mexico). The term is not usually applied to people from Spain, who are "Spanish."

Soda or Pop (In Boston it is "Tonic.")

- Any soft drink such as Coke, Fanta, Pepsi, 7-Up, etc.

Suspenders

- Used to hold up men's trousers.

Braces

- Metal work used to straighten teeth and done by a dentist.

Game Park

- Used as a playground with activities for children

Downtown

- The central part of a city, the business district of a city

Uptown

- Away from the city center, usually a residential area within the city limits

Inner city

- Usually the poorest section of the city and often with a high crime rate

I'm going to get a haircut today and look sharp.

- I'm going to a hair salon or to a hair stylist to get a new or better look.

These jeans are cool.

- The jeans are very fashionable / current.

Jimmy and his buddies.

That is cool.
- That is nice and I like it.

I'm cool.
- I'm doing fine.

She's cool.
- She's not upset over anything that happened.
- She's a nice person to know, fun.
- She is desirable.

Just be cool.
- It's okay; just relax, calm down, act normal.

She gave me the cold shoulder.
- She ignored me and did not want to talk to me.

That was cold.
- That was done without caring for your feelings, hurtful.

That was a cold-blooded crime (usually killing).
- It was a crime so bad it is hard to imagine the reasons behind it.

He was at the wrong place at the wrong time.
- He got in trouble because he made a wrong choice in being there.

Restroom
    The toilet in a public place

Men's Room

- Toilet facility (room) for men

Ladies' Room (often still called a "Powder Room")

- Toilet facility (room) for women

Bathroom

- Toilet and bath facility

Long-johns

- Full-length winter underwear that keeps you warm.

Porterjohn

- Toilets used at large gatherings outdoors or at construction sites.

The police pulled Alex over for drinking and driving.

- The police arrested Alex for D.U.I. (driving under the influence)

Roaches/Cockroaches

- Bugs (insects) found mostly in dirty places.

Can I have a drag?

- Can I smoke a puff of your cigarette?

Can I have a toke? (or "have a hit?")

- Can I smoke a puff of your marijuana cigarette ("joint" or "roach")?

Cigarette butts

- What is left of cigarette after being smoked

Clean your cigarette butts away from the table
- Remove the ashtray from the table and empty it.

He's a snake and will stab you in the back.
- He is someone who cannot be trusted.

She is kind of played out after all that work.
   She is very tired after working all day.

Women wear underwear in Ghana and men wear briefs or supporters.
- Also used- women wear pants and men wear shorts.

The president ordered federal offices to lower the flag to half-staff in honor of the senator.
- Flying the flag at half-staff (or "half-mast") shows respect for someone of importance who has recently died.

Just hang on, buddy!
- Don't be so impatient, take your time

She got in his face and then hit him with a glass.
- She became violent after confronting him.

The woman was a decoy to help capture the johns.
- She posed as a prostitute in order to catch men who employ prostitutes.

Whorehouse
- House of prostitution

You're shoving this down everyone's throat.

- You're forcing something on people (like ideas etc.) that they don't want.

I don't have that kind of dough.

- I do not have that kind of money.

The politician ran his campaign on a shoelace.

- He ran for election on a small amount of money. (In British terms, you "stand" for election.)

That will knock your socks off.

- You'll be amazed.

Your turn to bust a move!

- Your turn to show your dancing ability.

He's celebrating the big four-oh!

- He is celebrating his 40th birthday.

He is a good guy, and he will bend over backwards for you.

- He's a nice person and very dependable and trustworthy.

She will put her foot down.

- She will insist on doing it her way.

She has both feet on the ground.

- She is a very stable person.

The bosses should not deny anybody his overtime and that is cut and dried.

- There is no way for them to avoid paying overtime.

I'm caught up with all my bills.
- I have paid all my balances and have no debt.

That was baloney.
- It does not make any sense. (Usually: That just isn't true.)

I'm really bummed out.
- I'm upset.
- I'm depressed.

The firefighters and the city reached deal
- Their contract was approved.

When hell freezes over.
- It will never happen.

Going to the doctor can be nerve racking.
- Getting a diagnosis at a doctor can be stressfull.

The judge said, "I do this with a heavy heart."
- The judge was unhappy to do what he had to do.

They told us right off the bat.
- They didn't hesitate to tell us. They told us immediately.

They fired the teachers.
- The teachers lost their jobs.

All the workers had pink slips.
- Indicates that they lost their job.

A lot of people have a sinking feeling about the changes.
- Many people are nervous about what will be done.

She was trying to play me.
- She was trying to deceive me.

That was the final straw.
That was the last straw.
That was the straw that broke the camel's back.
- There were many prior problems, but this was the one that forced us to act.

I have worked hard for this company, but I'm just a number to them.
- No one recognizes me for all the hard work I do.

As Boomers age, more seniors are getting stoned.
- More seniors are using illegal drugs.

He felt she was man-bashing him.
- She was making bad remarks about him based on him being a male

Tenants lash out at business owner.
- Tenants became angry with business owner.

Eighty percent of the workers received layoff notices
- Eighty percent of employees lost their jobs.

She worked as a nanny while in college.
- She was employed full-time to care for children.

In high school, she worked as a babysitter.
- She took care of children when asked to for a short period of time.

That lawyer was ordered to pay $1,500 restitution for gouging clients.
- That lawyer over-charged his clients and had to repay the money.

I'll check back with you later.
- At the moment I am busy, but I'll see you when I'm free.

Go and rough him up.
- Abuse him physically.

He went haywire.
- When he heard the bad news, he acted in an abnormal manner. (out of control)

This is a witch hunt against me.
- Even though I've done nothing wrong, others are looking for anything they can use against me.

A cop saw the suspect and busted him.
- A police officer arrested the person who is now charged with the crime.

You're killing a lot of time these days. (You are wasting a lot of time these days.)
- You should get busy doing something worthwhile.

Bargain hunter
- A person who looks for the best prices.

She will rub it in.
- She will tease you about this and never let you forget it.

Couch potato
- A person that sits on the sofa watching television all day; a lazy person

A realtor showed the couple a house they might like to buy.
- A sales person helped the couple find a house.

Retiree
- A person who no longer works a regular job but lives off savings and pensions.

Yo-yo Dieting
- A diet plan that produces only temporary weight loss.

Get a one-way ticket.
- Leave and don't come back again.

My husband is a slob.
- My husband does not clean up after himself.

End of Saturday mail delivery in not a done deal
- In order to save the post office some money a discussion is taking place about discontinuing Saturday mail.

A bad hair day puts a woman in a blue mood.
- When a woman's hair looks bad, she is unhappy.

You're up to no good.
- I'm not sure if you are going to do the right thing.

Olu plays baseball in the Pee Wee Club
- Olu plays baseball for the children's' group

High rise
- Tall buildings, condos, apartment, etc.

He's a whistle blower, and the company broke the law when they fired him.
- He reported illegal activity the company was doing and they fired him.

The show needs some therapy.
- The show needs some drastic changes.

People are getting cranky.
- People are becoming angry and irritable.

Who dat?
- Who is this?

Going back in time

Back in the day
- Being nostalgic and reminiscing

I'm pumped (up)!

I'm stoked!
- I am ready, I'm really excited!

He's fired up.
- He's ready to go, excited.

An informant.
- One who gives information to the police, usually for money or special favors.

Private eye
- A person hired to investigate privately a wrong doing and paid by the person.

Don't talk to me like a big time boss.
- Don't act so superior to me.

The car is a piece of junk.
- The car no longer operates and is valuable only as scrap metal.

I heard she is practicing baby making.
- I heard she wants to get pregnant.

My mind is in a fog right now – I can't think of anything.
- My mind is blank now; I can't keep an open mind.

I bust my ass here!
- I work really hard and do the best I can!

Don't jinx us.

- Don't put a curse on us.

Part of the fun is watching the cheerleaders
- The cheerleaders are women who dance and lead others in cheering for a team.

Strip Club / Strip Joint
- A place where naked women perform.

You have a crappy job.
- Your job isn't great.

We were just being silly
- We were just joking, laughing, and having fun.

After living on the lam for three months, he was captured on Monday.
- After hiding for three months, he was caught.

That just sucks to me.
- That does not appeal to me .

Gerald often stirs the pot.
- Gerald likes to start trouble.

Mary came from a close-knit family.
- Mary's family has strong ties.

Well, the kicker is she never wanted that dress anyway.
- The surprise is that she didn't want that dress.

There are too many bums on the street.
- There are too many homeless people (or beggars) on the street.

He was the bail bondsman who posted the bond to get Freddy out of jail.
- He was the person who put up the money to get Freddy released while he waited for a trial.

Sadly, that didn't fly.
- Sadly, it didn't work.

It's creeping me out.
- It's making me nervous.

Dr. Aseidu says that the team went back on their word.
- They broke their promise.

- 1) Ernest, can you please pass me the salad dressing?
     Ernest, can you please pass me the salad cream?

2) Ackah, where can I find the can opener?
   Ackah, where can I find the tin cutter ?

3) Donald packed all his stuff in the suitcase and took off ..
   Donald packed all his belongings in the portmanteau and left..

4) Adelaide is a hang up lady
   Adelaide is always tired

5) The beam lights of tony's car is messed up
   The highlights of tony's car is dead.

6) Andrea ,when are you gonna fix the signal lights on your car before cops pull you over

   Andrea, when are you going to fix the travigator lights on your car before police stops you..

7) My friend Juanito cant stand the smell of moth balls .

   My friend Juanito can stand the smell of camphor.

8) Waxtuz has not gotten over the joy of hang over from the teams success from the play offs.

   Waxtuz hasn't gone over his happinesss from the success of his team in the knockout games

9) Happy Forth

   Happy forth of july. ie, Happy Independence day

10) Where is my booga rag / snot rag , Tom?

    Where is my handkerchief ,Tom?

11) Why do you cut me off whenever I talk to you?

    Why do you always stop me from talking ?

12) Hanna's car is a gas guzzler .

    Hanna's car consumes alot of petrol

13) Mary's flip flops are cute

    Mary's sandals are beautiful / nice

14) Jessica told me not to hire any fender bender lawyer to handle my case.

Jessica told me not to hire any incompetent lawyer to handle my case.

A region in the United States is known as a state.
- Accra, Ghana, in West Africa is known as a region, but New York in the United States is known as a state.

States are sometimes identified by their nicknames, especially within the state itself.
- Alabama: Yellowhammer State, Heart of Dixie, Camellia State
- Alaska: The Last Frontier
- Arizona: Grand Canyon State, Copper State
- Arkansas: The Natural State, Land of Opportunity, The Razorback State
- California: Golden State
- Colorado: Centennial State, Colorful Colorado
- Connecticut: Constitution State, Nutmeg State
- Delaware: First State, Diamond State, Blue Hen State, Small Wonder
- Florida: Sunshine State
- Georgia: Peach State, Empire of the South, Goober State
- Hawaii: Aloha State, Pineapple State
- Idaho: Gem State, Spud State
- Illinois: Prairie State, Land of Lincoln
- Indiana: Hoosier State
- Iowa: Hawkeye State
- Kansas: Sunflower State, Salt of the Earth
- Kentucky: Bluegrass State
- Louisiana: Pelican State, Sugar State
- Maine: Pine Tree State

- Maryland: Old Line State, Free State
- Massachusetts: Bay State, Old Colony State, The Spirit of America
- Michigan: Great Lakes State, Wolverine State
- Minnesota: North Star State, Gopher State, Land of 10,000 Lakes, Bread and Butter State
- Mississippi: Magnolia State
- Missouri: Show Me State
- Montana: Treasure State, Big sky State
- Nebraska: Cornhusker State
- Nevada: Silver State, Battle Born State, Sagebrush State
- New Hampshire: Granite State
- New Mexico: Land of Enrichment
- New York: empire State
- North Carolina: Tar Heel State, Old North State
- North Dakota: Peace Garden State, Flickertail State, Roughrider State
- Ohio: Buckeye State, Modern Mother of Presidents
- Oklahoma: Sooner State
- Oregon: Beaver State
- Pennsylvania: Keystone State, Quaker State
- Rhode Island: Ocean State, Little Rhody
- South Carolina: Palmetto State
- South Dakota: Coyote State, Mount Rushmore State
- Tennessee: Volunteer State, Big Bend State
- Texas: Lone Star State
- Utah: Beehive State
- Vermont: Green Mountain State

- Virginia: Old Dominion
- Washington: Evergreen State, Chinook State
- West Virginia: Mountain State
- Wisconsin: Badger State
- Wyoming: Equality State, Cowboy State

Exclamations

Americans have many ways of showing surprise. These are just a few of them.

Boy, oh boy.

Wow!

Holy shit!

Yeah, man.

Oh! Shit

Well, I'll be a son-of-a-bitch

Damn!

I'll be damned (darned).

Oh, man!

Get outta here!

Are you kidding me?

On the Job

First Shift 8:00 am to 5:00 pm

This is the most common work schedule.

Second Shift 3:00 pm to 11:00 pm
- People working late afternoon until 11:00 p.m.
- Blue collar job.

Third Shift 11:00 pm – 7:00 am
- This is often called the "graveyard shift" or "working nights."

Education Terms

Pre-school and Kindergarten
- For the youngest children, usually ages four and five.

Elementary school
- Grades 1–6 or 1–5

Middle school
- Grades 6–8

Junior High School
  Grades 7–9

High School
- Grades 9–12 or 10–12

Community College
- An associate's degree can be earned and transferred to further college/university

Colleges – Two Year Degree
- Do not offer PhD degrees

Universities / Colleges
- First year- Freshman
- Second year- Sophomore
- Third year – Junior
- Fourth year – Senior

Internship
- A new doctor serving an apprenticeship as an assistant resident at a hospital just after graduation from medical school.

Associate's program
- Two year program

Bachelor program
- Four year program

Master's Program

One or two year program after earning Bachelor's Degree

What is your major?
- What are you studying in college?

Doctoral Program
- Usually a longer period of years to earn the title "doctor" —*not* a medical doctor's program.

Alumnus/Alumna
- A man/woman who attended and (usually) graduated from a school, college, or university

Buying a Car

Auto/Automobile/Car/"Wheels"
- A means of transportation

Auto show
- Showing all types of cars

Auto repairman
- One who repairs damaged cars or cars needing repair

Auto salvage yard/Junkyard
- Where cars that are not usable are left and parts are salvaged

I'm going to trade in my old car.
- I'm going to use my old car as part payment toward a newer model.

How much are you looking to spend?
- What do you expect to pay for the car?

The car is fully loaded, has the whole nine yards.
- The car has all the gadgets like sound system, air conditioning (or "AC"), etc.

Be careful you don't buy a lemon.
- Don't buy a defective car with lots of problems.

That's my final offer. (I won't pay anymore than that.)

Money

- One penny: 1 cent
- Nickel: 5 cents
- Dime: 10 pennies
- Quarter: 25 pennies (Sometimes called "two bits.")
- Buck/Dollar Bill: One hundred cents or one hundred pennies - $1.00
- Five dollars: $5.00
- Ten dollars: $10.00
- Twenty dollars: $20.00 (Sometimes called a "saw-buck.")
- Fifty dollars - $50.00
- One hundred dollars - $100.00

Closing Comments

Thank you for reading this book. Put a smile on your face and God bless you.

www.ingramcontent.com/pod-product-compliance
Lightning Source LLC
LaVergne TN
LVHW041542060526
838200LV00037B/1095